BEGINNER'S GUIDE TO READING THE QUR'ĀN

AHMET BURSALI

Editor: Hüseyin Bingül
Art Director: Engin Çiftçi
Graphic Design & Layout by Şaban Kalyoncu, İhsan Demirhan, Hüseyin Kasımoğlu and İbrahim Akdağ

Published by Tughra Books
345 Clifton Ave., Clifton,
NJ, 07011, USA

www.tughrabooks.com

Library of Congress Cataloging-in-Publication Data Available

ISBN: 978-1-59784-273-0

Printed by
Görsel Dizayn Ofset Matbaacılık Tic.Ltd.Şti., İstanbul - Turkey
T: +90 212 671 91 00

("In the Name of Allāh, the All-Merciful, the All-Compassionate")

"The best among you are those who learn the Qur'ān and teach it to others."

(*Bukhārī*, "Fadāilu'l-Qur'ān," 21)

"Recite the Qur'ān, for it will come on the Day of Resurrection
to intercede for its companions."

(*Muslim*, "Salātu'l-Musafirīn," 252)

"The best word is Allāh's Book. The best path is Muhammad's path."

(*Muslim*, "Jumu'ah," 43)

"Recite the Qur'ān calmly and distinctly
(with your mind and heart concentrated on it)."

(al-Muzzammil 73:4)

ACKNOWLEDGMENTS

The preparation of this *Beginner's Guide to Reading the Qur'ān* would not have been possible without the valuable contributions of Mustafa Yiğit from Texas and Adem Başkaya from New Jersey, USA. I also would like to express my gratitude to Saber Abdelfattah from Egypt, who ably assisted me in providing all the examples from the Holy Qur'ān. I would particularly like to thank Mustafa Tezcan, the retired imâm of the Grand Çamlıca Mosque in Istanbul, Ali Demirel and Ismail Kayar for their valuable assistance and criticism to the text. I am also thankful to Nisa Nur Terzi for proofreading the text. I hope that this guide will serve as a valuable source for believers from all age groups in their quest for learning the recitation of the Holy Qur'ān.

TABLE OF CONTENTS

CHAPTER 2: INTRODUCTION TO QUR'ĀN RECITATION AND THE DAILY PRAYERS

"The best of my community are those who memorize and serve the Qur'ān."

(*Tabarānī*, Mu'jamu'l-Kabīr, 12/125)

FOREWORD

All praise and gratitude is to our Lord Who sent us the Holy Qur'ān as the blessed life-guide with which we feel honored to comply. May the most perfect greetings and blessings of Allāh be upon our Prophet, the Best of Creation, by means of whom only can we understand the Divine Message of the Qur'ān in depth and learn how to read and recite it with correct pronunciation and methods of recitation.

What meaning would the Book of the Qur'ān have without its addressee—the man? And what meaning would man actually have without the guidance of the Qur'ān? So, reading and reciting the Qur'ān, comprehending and practicing it in everyday life should be the essential objective of all believers. Though this is primarily a personal responsibility, transferring it all along the ages has been reckoned as a holy mission by all Qur'ān lovers. As an explicit manifestation of this unique understanding, the righteous followers of our beloved Prophet, may Allāh be pleased with them all, initiated "the science of Qur'ān recitation" as a substantive scientific study, with the intention of handing the Holy Qur'ān down to us with the original form as it was brought by Gabriel, the angel of Revelation, to our Prophet Muhammad, peace and blessings be upon him. Having composed numerous works in the field thus far, these righteous followers of the Prophet have set forth their sincere resolution and benevolence. No doubt, the prolific efforts pertaining to this blessed field shall persevere until the end of time.

As expressed in the hadīth above, our humble intention in setting out to prepare this work is to contribute to the existing works that have been produced to teach how to recite the Qur'ān—to be at the service of which we regard the raison d'être of our lives—to new generations, and to meet the basic needs of many people wishing to learn how to recite the Qur'ān accurately.

In this guide, taking the novice Qur'ān readers into consideration, we have had a focused concern for the following principles:

- Those who shall study this guide will be people from all ages—young and adult alike.

- This work will essentially be utilized by those who have just started learning how to recite the Qur'ān.

- Instead of contenting with just a few examples for each topic, we have preferred to provide the students with enough examples to practice, which promises to make a significant contribution for a better comprehension.

- Almost all the exercises have been quoted directly from the Qur'ān.

- Every single topic has been supported by visual aids in order to help the learners to better understand them.

- Topics in this work have been presented in order of difficulty so that learners accumulate newer knowledge by building on the previously learnt ones.

- This work consists mainly of two parts:
  - recognition and articulation of letters
  - learning to recite the Qur'ān and perform the daily Prayers.

- Although reciting the Qur'ān is in itself an act of worship and its reward is manifold, reciting a portion from the Qur'ān is necessary while performing the daily Prayers. Therefore, the ultimate goal of every single Qur'ān learner should be to learn performing the Prayers accurately. We have therefore included in the second part of this guide related topics such as short *sūrahs* and the prayers, glorifications recited after the Daily Prayers, as well as the first and second calls to the Prayer.

- It is possible that some points may have escaped our attention and been left inarticulate in spite of all our effort. Therefore, we would be grateful if the readers would indicate any mistakes or omissions in the text. All the beauty and perfection belong to our Lord, whereas flaws belong to us. May our Lord grant all our brothers and sisters the blessing of learning and reciting the Qur'ān.

RECOMMENDATIONS FOR STUDENTS AND TUTORS

It is highly recommended to study this guide with a tutor and thus learn to read the Qur'ān with practice under the monitoring of a teacher or tutor. Considering the fact that every Qur'ān learner may not have the opportunity to attend a class or find a tutor to learn and practice the Qur'ān recitation, we have made an extra effort to design this guide in a style enabling self-directed learning. The Qur'ān learner should not, however, rely solely on him or herself in learning the recitation of the Qur'ān. The following issues are noteworthy for both the tutors and students:

It is essential that every believing man and woman learn to read and recite the Holy Qur'ān, which is revealed in Arabic. As it is the case with all other languages, the Arabic language has distinctive phonetic features. In addition, the ideal time to acquire the articulation (or correct pronunciation) of phonemes in any particular language is the period of childhood. Indeed, the voice organ and the articulation mechanisms of a child develop along with the physical growth; and when one reaches the teenage years, the laryngeal anatomy and physiology as well as the articulation of sounds in his or her language becomes settled and steady. For this very reason, in case one comes up with the sound system of a different language after puberty, it may be difficult to articulate precise pronunciations of some sounds of the new language. Though it is not with all the phonemes, this difficulty may happen with at least certain phonemes, with a variance depending on different mother languages.

This is of course a natural case for all languages. Overcoming this common problem is yet possible through the guidance of a tutor, with plenty of exercise. Throughout the history of learning to read and recite the Qur'ān, Muslims have developed many varying methods. The experiences that have been accumulated so far indicate that the most effective and healthy learning method is based upon two elements:

i)   listening to the expert tutor,

ii) presenting the learned material back to the tutor for correction, over and over again until one achieves correct recitation, giving each phoneme its full value.

Reciting the Qur'ān to a knowing companion, an elder sibling or someone in the community is another means of avoiding errors. In this way, the Qur'ān students can test their recitation by reciting the Qur'ān to a companion who is knowledgeable enough to recognize errors. In case one does not have any of these opportunities, there is no any other alternative than independent or self-directed learning. This is a situation mostly observed in non-Muslim countries where it is difficult, but not impossible, to study the recitation of the Qur'ān under the monitoring of a tutor. Still, an expert tutor should be sought as much as possible, and it should be known that independent or self-directed learning is the last method to be applied. Another point facilitating learning and making it permanent is to do repeated oral exercises. As it happens in many other learning activities, the contribution of repeated practice and abundant exercises to learning is an obvious fact.

Another advise to the new learners of the Qur'ān is to listen to the recitation of the *qāris* (reciters of the Qur'ān) and the *hāfizes* (who have memorized the entire Qur'ān and thus recite it by heart in style) as well as their audio and video cassettes, VCDs and DVDs, or to make frequent use of the educational recitation activities offered by audio-visual materials, such as VCDs, DVDs or websites. Forming such a good habit shall surely be an attitude that keeps alive, consolidates and advances the quality of Qur'ān recitation.

Throughout this work, we have deliberately avoided the transliterations of prayers, supplications, and the verses from the Qur'ān. The reason of this is that if the Arabic phonemes are not pronounced correctly during their recitation, the meaning may completely change and thus be distorted. And that may cause the risk that a person may have a life-long habit of incorrect recitation. These pronunciation errors may become so fixed in the learners' Qur'ān recitation that the fossilized pronunciation errors cannot often be changed despite all the hard work and conscious efforts. Besides, if that incorrect recitation takes place during the daily Prayers, this may put the acceptability of the Prayers at risk as the meanings might change. This issue stands as one of the vital points for both the tutors and learners of Qur'ān recitation, which in other words denotes a heavy responsibility for all. In a nutshell, instead of easy but risky ways, the precise and healthy methods should be preferred.

To give good news to the learners of the Qur'ān, we would like to emphasize here the fact that a short period of no more than a month shall be enough to learn reading the Qur'ān if the program is followed with a vivid motivation, focused attention and resolution. Indeed, Allāh the Almighty has made the Qur'ān easy to learn both to read and to recite. Therefore, following this initial study of about a month, one can easily advance his or her recitation of the Qur'ān by learning the further details of recitation by means of the assistance of the expert teachers.

The last but not the least important point is that the process of learning the Qur'ān recitation penetrates all along one's life by its positive and negative aspects. In the end, one keeps the fossilized recitation errors all along his or her life if he or she has learned it incorrectly or pronounced the Qur'anic words without giving each phoneme its full value. Fully aware of this general situation, each and every Qur'ān student ought to make an effort to learn reciting the Qur'ān in the most beautiful and precise style considering the time and energy spent for this blessed activity.

"O my Lord! Ease my task, and do not harden!
O my Lord! Let my task be completed in good!"

CHAPTER 1

RECOGNITION AND ARTICULATION OF LETTERS

Section 1: Recognition of Letters and Sounds

The Qur'ān is revealed in Arabic. It is essential, therefore, that every believing man and woman first learn the Arabic letters and sounds in order to recite the Qur'ān correctly. While reciting the Qur'ān is itself a meritorious act of worship, each and every Muslim has to recite a portion from the Qur'ān in their Daily Prayers (*Salāh*).

In relation to the rewards of reciting the Qur'ān, Prophet Muhammad, peace and blessings be upon him, said: "Whoever reads **a letter** from the Book of Allāh, he or she will be credited with **a reward** for that good, righteous deed, and (bear in mind that) the reward of a good, righteous deed will be multiplied by ten. I am not saying that '*alif-lām-mīm*' is a letter, rather I am saying that '*alif*' is a (single) letter, '*lām*' is a letter, and '*mīm*' is a letter. So increase your recitation of the Qur'ān to gain these rewards, and to gain the following reward as well." He also said: "As for the one who (is not well-versed in the Arabic language and thus) recites with difficulty, then he or she will have **twice that reward**." (*Tirmidhī, 3/164; Bukhārī, 60/459*)

ARABIC ALPHABET

The Arabic alphabet has 28 letters and is written and read from the right to the left. Arabic alphabet is consonant-based, and each consonantal letter is read with an inherent "a" sound. This "a" sound of the consonantal letters can be articulated with either the soft "a" or the hard "a". Therefore;

- The letters written in **black** below are soft, and the "a" in these soft letters is sounded as the "a" in *cat* or *baby*.

- The letters written in red are hard, and the "a" in these hard letters is sounded as the "a" in *car* or *cup*.

- The letters written in blue are sounded sometimes as soft, sometimes as hard. Bear in mind that " لا " in this category is not a single letter on its own but a joint form of the letters " ل " and " ا ".

- Please repeat all the letters below until you articulate the sounds of the letters in the most precise way.

ج جيم	ث ثا	ت تا	ب با	اءٔ ألف
ر را	ذ ذال	د دال	خ خا	ح حا
ض ضاد	ص صاد	ش شين	س سين	ز زاى
ف فا	غ غين	ع عين	ظ ظا	ط طا
ن نون	م ميم	ل لام	كٔ كاف	ق قاف
	ى يا	لا لام ألف	و واو	ه ها

LETTERS WITH SIMILAR SOUNDS BUT VARYING PRONUNCIATIONS

- The following letters may sound similar. However, both their written forms and pronunciations are different from each other. They fall into the following six main categories.

- Please practice the group of letters in each category separately, concentrating on one group of letters at a time. Please do not move to the next group of letters before perfecting the articulation of each letter. Only after you finish reading the group of letters in a particular category correctly, you can practice reading the letters of the next category.

- As some of these phonemes may not have a sound-for-sound counter in your native language, you ought to practice the pronunciation of every single phoneme until your tutor approves of your articulation.

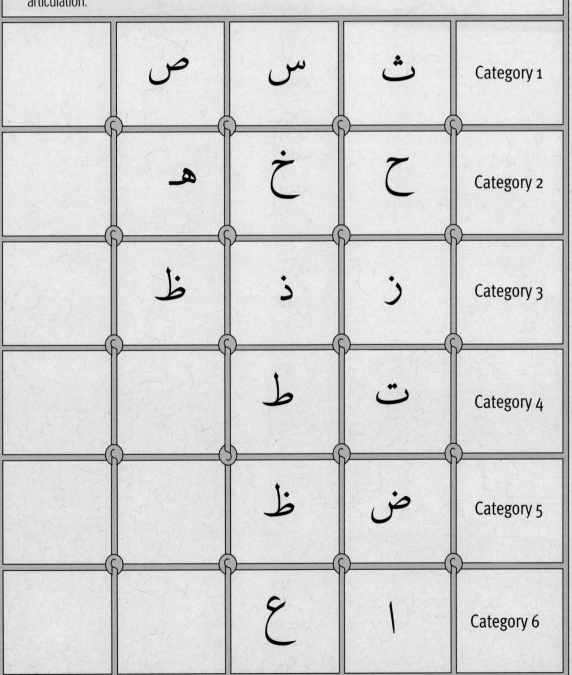

	ص	س	ث	Category 1
	هـ	خ	ح	Category 2
	ظ	ذ	ز	Category 3
		ط	ت	Category 4
		ظ	ض	Category 5
		ع	ا	Category 6

RECOGNITION OF LETTERS IN INITIAL, MEDIAL, AND FINAL POSITIONS

- Most of the Arabic letters are written in distinct forms when they are connected with a preceding and/or a succeeding letter, depending on whether they are at the beginning, middle, or end of a word.
- Only six letters are not connected (in writing) with the succeeding letter. These six letters are printed in blue below.
- All the letters with their written form in initial, medial and final positions are presented in alphabetical order below.

ج	ث	ت	ب	ءا
ج ج ج	ث ث ث	ت ت ت	ب ب ب	ا ئ ا
ر	ذ	د	خ	ح
ر ر ر	ذ ذ ذ	د د د	خ خ خ	ح ح ح
ض	ص	ش	س	ز
ض ض ض	ص ص ص	ش ش ش	س س س	ز ز ز
ف	غ	ع	ظ	ط
ف ف ف	غ غ غ	ع ع ع	ظ ظ ظ	ط ط ط
ن	م	ل	ك	ق
ن ن ن	م م م	ل ل ل	ك ك ك	ق ق ق
ى	لا	و	ه	
ي ي ى	لا لا لا	و و و	ه ه ه	

SECTION 2: ARTICULATION OF LETTERS WITH SHORT VOWELS

Arabic, which is a consonant-based language, does not have vowels as letters. Therefore, the short vowels are shown with supplemental diacritical signs placed over or under the consonants. Any of these diacritical vowel signs placed over or under a consonant is called *harakah* (plural *harakāt*).

ARTICULATION OF LETTERS BY *FAT-HAH* (＿ THE VOWEL SIGN FOR "A")

- *Fat-hah* is one of these vowel signs, or *harakāt*, and it gives a closed "a" sound (as in c**a**p, h**a**t, m**a**tch, or s**a**ck) to the soft consonants, and an open "a" sound (as in c**a**rp, h**u**t, m**a**rch, or s**u**ck) to the hard ones.
- The sign of *Fat-hah* (＿) is a small straight line inclined down towards its left end and is put over the consonants.
- Please see how the isolated letters in blue are connected with a preceding and/or a succeeding letter in each box below.
- The *fat-hah* signs placed over the consonants are in red color. Please pay attention to the pronunciation of words with the *fat-hah* sign.

سَ كَ نَ	بَ عَ ثَ	خَ رَ جَ	كَ تَ بَ
سَكَنَ	بَعَثَ	خَرَجَ	كَتَبَ
اَ مَ رَ	ضَ رَ بَ	حَ مَ لَ	خَ لَ قَ
اَمَرَ	ضَرَبَ	حَمَلَ	خَلَقَ
صَ بَ رَ	سَ اَ لَ	فَ تَ حَ	غَ فَ رَ
صَبَّرَ	سَاَلَ	فَتَحَ	غَفَرَ
ذَ هَ بَ	فَ عَ لَ	ذَ رَ اَ	حَ سَ دَ
ذَهَبَ	فَعَلَ	ذَرَاَ	حَسَدَ
بَ دَ اَ	اَ خَ ذَ	تَ رَ كَ	وَ لَ دَ
بَدَاَ	اَخَذَ	تَرَكَ	وَلَدَ
عَ بَ دَ	صَ دَ قَ	سَ كَ تَ	شَ رَ حَ
عَبَدَ	صَدَقَ	سَكَتَ	شَرَحَ

ARTICULATION OF LETTERS BY *KASRAH* (ِ THE VOWEL SIGN FOR *"i"*)

- *Kasrah*, another vowel sign, or *harakah*, gives a closed "i" sound (as in ship, sit, honey, or journey) to the soft consonants. In the hard consonants, however, this *kasrah* sign is pronounced like the unrounded *schwa* sound, which is the most common English vowel sound (as in family, cousin, pencil, basket, or jacket).
- The *kasrah* sign (ِ) is a small straight line inclined down towards its left end and is put under the consonants.
- Please see how the isolated letters in blue are connected with a preceding and/or a succeeding letter in each box below.
- *Kasrah* signs are given in red color. Please pay attention to the pronunciation of words with the *kasrah* sign.

عَ لِ مَ	سَ مِ عَ	وَ سِ عَ	حَ بِ طَ
عَلِمَ	سَمِعَ	وَسِعَ	حَبِطَ
أَ بَ تِ	شَ هِ دَ	عَ مِ لَ	حَ سِ بَ
أَبَتِ	شَهِدَ	عَمِلَ	حَسِبَ
عَ هِ دَ	شَ رِ بَ	وَ رَثَ ةِ	أَ ذِ نَ
عَهِدَ	شَرِبَ	وَرَثَةِ	أَذِنَ
تَ جِ دَ	أَ زِ فَ	حَ مِ دَ	رَ حِ مَ
تَجِدَ	أَزِفَ	حَمِدَ	رَحِمَ
بَ خِ لَ	رَ دِ فَ	تَ بِ عَ	خَ شِ یَ
بَخِلَ	رَدِفَ	تَبِعَ	خَشِیَ
رَ ضِ یَ	خَ طِ فَ	أَ مِ نَ	عِ وَ جَ
رَضِیَ	خَطِفَ	أَمِنَ	عِوَجَ

ARTICULATION OF LETTERS BY *DHAMMAH* (ُـ THE VOWEL SIGN FOR "*U*")

- *Dhammah* is another vowel sign (ُ) which is similar to a large comma or a small curl-like diacritic placed above the consonants and is pronounced by rounding the lips. The *dhammah* sign gives a closed, front "u" sound (as in tube, Munich, or Düsseldorf) to the soft consonants while it gives a closed, back "u" sound (as in full, put or book) to the strong ones.
- Please see how the isolated letters in blue are connected with a preceding and/or a succeeding letter in each box below.
- *Dhammah* signs are given in red color. Please pay attention to the pronunciation of words with the *dhammah* sign.

خُ لِ قَ	اُ ذِ نَ	ظُ لِ مَ	وُ لِ دَ
خُلِقَ	اُذِنَ	ظُلِمَ	وُلِدَ
اُ فِ كَ	كُ تِ بَ	خُ بُ ثَ	هُ دِ ىَ
اُفِكَ	كُتِبَ	خُبُثَ	هُدِى
تُ طِ عِ	صُ حُ فُ	حَ سُ نَ	یَ لِ دُ
تُطِعِ	صُحُفُ	حَسُنَ	یَلِدُ
نَ رِ ثُ	یَ لِ جُ	ذُ بِ حَ	وُ ضِ عَ
نَرِثُ	یَلِجُ	ذُبِحَ	وُضِعَ
حُ شِ رَ	ذُ كِ رَ	عُ رِ ضَ	خُ مُ سَ هُ
حُشِرَ	ذُكِرَ	عُرِضَ	خُمُسَهُ
وُ عِ دَ	كُ تِ بِ هِ	اُ خِ ذَ	قُ ضِ ىَ
وُعِدَ	كُتِبِهِ	اُخِذَ	قُضِى

ASSORTED EXERCISES (1)

• Please recite carefully the following examples from the Qur'ān that contain *fat-hah*, *kasrah* and *dhammah*.

عُفِىَ	جَعَلَ	اُخَرَ	كَمَثَلِ
حَضَرَ	وَمَثَلُ	كَتَمَ	سَفِهَ
سَالَكَ	لَهُ	حَذَرَ	اَفَلَ
وَقُضِىَ	رَفَثَ	فَرَضَ	هِىَ
فَصَلَ	قَدَرُهُ	اَجَلَهُ	فَبَعَثَ
وَجَدَ	بِيَدِكَ	وَهُوَ	وَقَتَلَ
ضَعُفَ	وَحَسُنَ	كَثُرَ	دَخَلَهُ

SECTION 3: JOINING AND DOUBLING LETTERS

ARTICULATION OF JOINED LETTERS BY *JAZM* (ْ COMBINER)

- The *jazm* sign (ْ) is a small circle-shaped diacritic placed above a letter. It combines or joins the letter it stands above to the previous letter to form one syllable. A letter with a *jazm* makes the letter silent; that is, the letter is read without any vowel when it is joined to the preceding letter.
- *Jazm* sign may occur in the middle or at the end of a word. It never occurs above the letters in the beginning.
- *Jazm* signs are in red color below. Please study each word and read them aloud clearly and one by one.

قُلْ	هُمْ	لَمْ	كُلْ
تُبْ	ذُقْ	زِدْ	عَنْ
لَكُمْ	اَرْسَلَ	اَمْ	زُرْتُمْ
بَعْدَ	قَبْلَ	اِلَيْكَ	عَلَيْكَ
قُمْ	يَعْلَمُ	اَنْتَ	كُنْتَ
عَلَيْكُمْ	اَنْتُمْ	مِنْكُمْ	نَعْبُدُ

19

ASSORTED EXERCISES (2)

• Please recite carefully the following examples from the Qur'ān with *jazm*.

اَنْفُسَهُمْ	كَيْدَهُمْ	يُدْخِلْهُ	عَنْهُمْ
وَنِعْمَ	مِنْ اَهْلِكَ	غَدَوْتَ	اِنْ تَمْسَسْكُمْ
مِنْ حَوْلِكَ	فَمِنْ نَفْسِكَ	اَمْ حَسِبْتُمْ	مَنْ يُطِعِ
اَجْرُهُمْ	سَنَكْتُبُ	اَقْرَبُ	وَلْيَعْلَمَ
اَنْ يَنْكِحَ	وَاَخَذْنَ	اِذْ لَمْ اَكُنْ	تَرْكَنَ
اَلَمْ تَرَ	وَمَنْ يُشْرِكْ	وَيَغْفِرُ	اَصْدَقُ
اَنْعَمَ	وَعِظْهُمْ	فَلَنْ تَجِدَ	اُنْظُرْ كَيْفَ

ARTICULATION OF LETTERS BY *SHADDAH* (ﱞ DOUBLING LETTER SIGN)

- The *shaddah* (ﱞ) is a diacritic shaped like an upside down "m" that is put over the letter. *Shaddah* is to make the letter (with the *shaddah* sign over it) to be pronounced twice by joining and doubling at the same time. Therefore,

  a) The *shaddah* sign first joins in pronunciation the letter above which it occurs to the preceding letter.

  b) The letter above which the *shaddah* sign occurs is then repeated (or doubled) and pronounced with its own vowel with a strong emphasis.

- When a *shaddah* is used over a consonant which also has a *fat-hah* or *dhammah* sign (ﱞ), the *fat-hah* or *dhammah* is written above the *shaddah* sign, while a *kasrah* is written below the consonant.

- Please pay attention to the individual letters in the first two lines given in blue and see how the *shaddah* sign makes up the recitation of letters.

- Please recite the words one by one and clearly; pay attention to the effect of the *shaddah*, placing a strong emphasis on the letter it doubles.

رَ بْ بَ هُ مْ	اِ نْ نَ كَ	اِ نْ نَ	اَ وْ وَ لَ
رَبَّهُمْ	اِنَّكَ	اِنَّ	اَوَّلَ
ثُ مْ مَ	حَ رْ رَ مَ	نَ زْ زَ لَ	دَ مْ مَ رَ
ثُمَّ	حَرَّمَ	نَزَّلَ	دَمَّرَ
طَهِّرْ	فَسَبِّحْ	فَكَبِّرْهُ	رَبّْ
حَقَّ	كَلَّمَ	فَضَّلَ	جَهَنَّمَ
شَرَّ	زَيَّنَ	فَكَّرَ	رَبُّكَ

SECTION 4: PROLONGATION AND ARTICULATION OF *MADD* (PROLONGED) LETTERS

- The word *madd* (literally "stretching") means a prolongation or extension to the duration of the letters of *madd*. There are three **madd (prolonged) letters**: the bare *alif*, the bare **waw**, the bare **yā**. They are called "bare" since they do not have any *harakah*, or vowel sign above or under them. These letters make the vowel signs (*harakah*) of the preceding consonant to be recited longer than the normal, just like having an exaggerated, over-emphasized tone with a slight hint of attitude when speaking. For example: "He is far f**aa**r away," "I am way w**aa**y ahead of time," and "Where have you b**ee**n?"
- Prolonging a *madd* letter to the required length is achieved by using the standard length of "two *harakah*s." In other words, the *madd* (prolonged) letters are lengthened for the duration of "two *harakah*s" (which is about 2-3 seconds). Accordingly, the vowel of the preceding consonant to be prolonged for the duration of two *harakah*s is lengthened in recitation for about 2-3 seconds more than the normal recitation. The best example illustrating the prolongation of these three letters is the word أُوتِينَا.

LESSON 11 – *ALIF MADD* (PROLONGING *ALIF* – ا)

- The bare *alif* (without any *harakah*, or vowel sign, over or below it) always occurs after the sign of *fathah*. The vowel of the preceding letter is prolonged for the duration of two *harakah*s (2-3 seconds).
- Please recite the following examples one by one and clearly; pay attention to the prolonged *alif* letters.

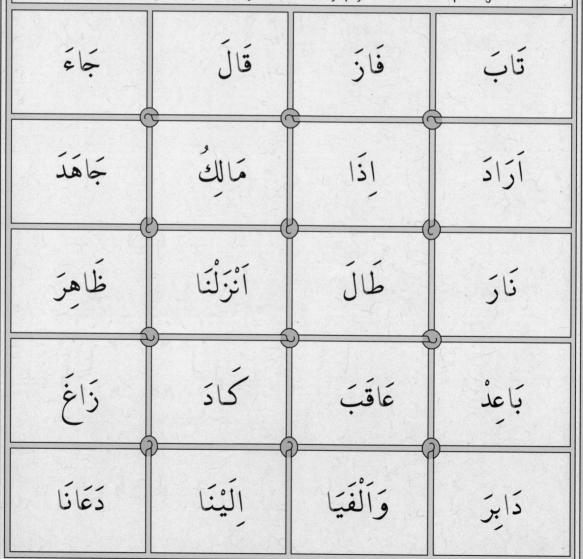

تَابَ	فَازَ	قَالَ	جَاءَ
اَرَادَ	اِذَا	مَالِكُ	جَاهَدَ
نَارَ	طَالَ	اَنْزَلْنَا	ظَاهِرَ
بَاعِدْ	عَاقَبَ	كَادَ	زَاغَ
دَابِرَ	وَالْفَيَا	اِلَيْنَا	دَعَانَا

WAW MADD (PROLONGING WAW – و)

- The prolonging **waw** occurs after the sign of *dhammah* over it and prolongs the vowel of the preceding letter for the duration of two *harakah*s (2-3 seconds).
- Please examine the following words containing the prolonging *waw*.
- Please recite the following examples one by one and clearly, paying attention to prolonging *waw* letters.

يَقُولُ	اَعُوذُ	اُدْعُوا	تُوبُوا
يَعْقُوب	مُفْلِحُونَ	يَشْكُرُونَ	وَيَبْغُونَ
يُوقِنُونَ	يَرْجُوا	يَكُونُ	تُبْعَثُونَ
يُجَاهِدُونَ	يَتُوبُ	عَابِدُونَ	يَكْفُرُونَ
كَافِرُونَ	خَاسِرُونَ	صَابِرُونَ	تَصِفُونَ
نُورُهُمْ	تُوعَدُونَ	يَقُولُ	صُدُورُهُمْ

23

YĀ MADD (PROLONGING YĀ – ى)

- The prolonging *yā* occurs mostly after the sign of *kasrah* below the preceding letter and prolongs the vowel of this preceding letter for the duration of two *harakah*s (2-3 seconds).
- Please examine the following words containing the prolonging *yā*.
- Please recite the following examples one by one and clearly, paying attention to prolonging *yā* letters.

فَاَمَّا الْيَتِيمَ	يُرِيدُ	نَعِيمُ	قِيلَ
اَبِى	اَبَابِيلَ	يُحْيِيكُمْ	فِيهِ
تَمِيلُ	نَصِيبُ	اَطِيعُونَ	يُقِيمُونَ
تُثِيرُ	نُرِيدُ	مُخْلِصِينَ	يُصِيبُ
اِيمَانَكُمْ	غِيظَ	تَرْمِيهِمْ	يُعْطِيكَ
رُسُلِى	اُجِيبُ	نَفْسِى	تُثِيرُ

24

THE STRETCHING *MADD* SIGN

- The stretching *madd* sign (‑ᷱ‑) is written as a short vertical stroke placed over or below a letter. The stretching *madd* sign makes the letter be recited 2-3 seconds longer than normal articulation of that letter and thus is prolonged for the duration of two *harakah*s.

- When the stretching *madd* sign occurs over a letter, it makes the duration of the letter prolonged for the duration of two *harakah*s (2-3 seconds) with the vowel "*a*" (as in c**a**r, sc**a**rf, or l**au**gh); if the sign is below a letter, it prolongs the letter with the vowel "*ī*" (as in sh**ee**p or b**ee**f).

- The stretching *madd* sign makes the letter it occurs be recited longer, regardless of whether or not there exists one of the prolonged *(madd)* letters (i.e. the bare *alif*, the bare *waw*, or the bare *yā*) above the following letter.

تَعَالٰى	طٰهٰ	اٰتَيْنَاهُ	اَللّٰهُ
فِيهَا	اِبْرٰهِيمَ	ذٰلِكَ	اٰمَنَ
هٰذَا	الْهُكُمْ	فِيهِ	اِسْحٰقَ
اِنّٖى	اِلٰى	مُوسٰى	اِسْمٰعِيلَ
اَخٖى	هٰرُونَ	بَشِيرٌ	سُلَيْمٰنَ
عِيسٰى	خَبِيرٌ	اَبِيكُمْ	وَقِيلَ

ASSORTED EXERCISES (3)

- Please recite carefully the following examples from the Qur'ān that contain *madd (prolonged) letters, stretching madd signs* and *doubling letters by shaddah*.

حَدِيثٌ	لَا يَمُوتُ	يُوقِنُونَ	اٰيَاتِنَا
وَيُمِيتُ	اَبْوَابَ	خَالِدِينَ	يَتَفَكَّرُونَ
يَسِيرُوا	اٰمِنِينَ	وَيُرِيكُمْ	مِنْ مَحَارِيبَ
وَتَمَاثِيلَ	لَا يَمْلِكُونَ	فِيهِمَا	يُنَادِيهِمْ
اَلَّذِينَ	اٰنَسْتُ	اٰتِيكُمْ	فَاَسْكَنَّاهُ
اَفَلَا تَتَّقُونَ	بِمَا كَذِبُونِ	دَمَّرْنَاهُمْ	يَتَطَهَّرُونَ
لَا يُوَلُّونَ	وَمَا تَلَبَّثُوا	صَيَاصِيهِمْ	يُصَلِّى

SECTION 5: ARTICULATION OF LETTERS WITH *TANWĪN* (NUNATION)

- *Tanwīn*, or **nunation**, is indicated by doubling the three vowel signs at the end of the word. These signs of *double fat-hah* (ً), *double kasrah* (ٍ), and *double dhammah* (ٌ) are called **tanwīn**, or **nunation**, signs.

- Nunations occur only at the end of words; the words with *nunation* end in the consonant "-n" of the ن (*nun*) letter. Therefore, the three *nunation* signs indicate that the short vowels "a," "i," or "u" are followed by the consonant "-n."

- Nunated letters are recited with the sounds "**an**" (as in b**an**, sp**an**, s**un**, or b**un**), "**in**" (as in pidg**in**, sk**in**, or verm**in**), or "(o)**un**" (as in n**oun** or Sams**un**). Here, please take care not to lengthen the vowel that comes before the consonant "-n." One of the best examples for the last category with a short "**u**" vowel is رُسُلٌ.

LESSON 16 – NUNATION WITH DOUBLE *FAT-HAH* (ً)

- Please recite the following words, paying attention to the examples without the *nunation* in the first two lines given in blue and see how *nunation with double fat-hah* makes up the recitations of letters below.

عِلْمَنْ	دِينَنْ	بَصِيرَنْ	رِزْقَنْ
عِلْمًا	دِينًا	بَصِيرًا	رِزْقًا
نُورَنْ	هُودَنْ	أَبَدَنْ	حَسَنَتَنْ
نُورًا	هُودًا	أَبَدًا	حَسَنَةً
سَلَامًا	عُدْوَانًا	كَرِيمًا	كِتَابًا
مَاءً	عَذَابًا	كَثِيرًا	عَزِيزًا
غَفُورًا	قَوْمًا	جَمِيعًا	أَبْوَابًا

LESSON
17

NUNATION WITH DOUBLE *DHAMMAH* (ٌ)

- Please see the words with *nunation by double dhammah* in the following examples.
- Please pay attention to the examples without the *nunation* in the first two lines given in blue and see how *nunation with double dhammah* makes up the recitations of letters below.
- Please recite the following words containing *nunation*s *with double dhammah* one by one and clearly.

رُسُلٌ	اَحَدٌ	شَىْءٌ	حَقٌّ
رُسُلُ	اَحَدُ	شَىْءُ	حَقُّ
فَصَبْرٌ	اَلِيمٌ	شَدِيدٌ	صُمٌّ
فَصَبْرُ	اَلِيمُ	شَدِيدُ	صُمُّ
بُكْمٌ	رَحِيمٌ	شَاكِرٌ	عَزِيزٌ
خَيْرٌ	نُورٌ	غَفُورٌ	شَكُورٌ
مُبِينٌ	بَشِيرٌ	بَصِيرٌ	جَنَّةٌ
اَزْوَاجٌ	شِفَاءٌ	مُؤْصَدَةٌ	لِبَاسٌ

28

NUNATION WITH DOUBLE *KASRAH* (ٍ)

- Please see the words with **nunation by double kasrah** in the following examples.
- Please pay attention to the examples without the *nunation* in the first two lines given in blue and see how **nunation with double kasrah** makes up the recitations of letters below.
- Please recite the following words containing *nunations with double kasrah* one by one and clearly.

عِلْمٍ	مَسَدٍ	اَجْرٍ	جَنَّاتٍ
عِلْمٍ	مَسَدٍ	اَجْرٍ	جَنَّاتٍ
بِسَلَامٍ	اَحَدٍ	جُوعٍ	صِرَاطٍ
بِسَلَامٍ	اَحَدٍ	جُوعٍ	صِرَاطٍ
جَبَلٍ	هُمَزَةٍ	خَوْفٍ	قُرَيْشٍ
نَارٍ	هَادٍ	لَهَبٍ	اَمْرٍ
وَنَقْصٍ	عَدْنٍ	ذِكْرٍ	لَوْحٍ
حَاسِدٍ	رِجْزٍ	وَالِدٍ	سُنْدُسٍ

ASSORTED EXERCISES (4)

• Please recite carefully the following examples from the Qur'ān that contain *nunations*.

وَلَيَالٍ عَشْرٍ	حُبًّا جَمًّا	اَبِى لَهَبٍ	مِنْ جُوعٍ
شَيْطَانٍ رَجِيمٍ وَشَاهِدٍ وَمَشْهُودٍ	عَيْنٌ جَارِيَةٌ	رَاضِيَةً مَرْضِيَّةً	
وَنَفُورٍ	قَوْلًا سَدِيدًا	مُسْتَبْشِرَةٌ	ضَاحِكَةٌ
بَاطِلٌ	قَوْلًا مَيْسُورًا	عُلُوًّا	مَنَّاعٍ
فَتْحٌ قَرِيبٌ	عَدُوٌّ مُبِينٌ	نَاصِحٌ اَمِينٌ	مُتَبَّرٌ
حَمِيمٍ	مُسْتَقِيمٍ	صِرَاطٍ	دِينًا قَيِّمًا
كَفَّارٌ	سَحِيقٍ	مَكَانٍ	بَلْدَةٌ طَيِّبَةٌ

SECTION 6: EXTRA PROLONGATION (ٓ)

THE SIGN OF LONGER *MADD* (EXTRA PROLONGATION)

- When ***the wavy sign of longer madd*** (ٓ) occurs above a letter, that letter is recited 3-5 seconds longer than usual and can thus be prolonged up to four to six *harakah*s (about 5 seconds).
- The wavy sign of longer *madd* occurs always over the letters and prolongs the articulation of all three vowel signs (of *fat-hah*, *kasrah*, and *dhammah*).
- Please recite the following words, paying attention to the necessary extra prolongations.

جَآءَ	مَآ اَعْبُدُ	سُوٓءَ	سِيٓءَ
جِيٓءَ	حَدَآئِقَ	سَآءَ	مَشَّآءٍ
اَلَّذِيٓ اَطْعَمَهُمْ	رَبَّنَآ اٰمَنَّا	شُهَدَآءَ	اَبْنَآءَ
اِعْلَمُوٓا اَنَّمَا	خَلَٓائِفَ	كَآفَّةً	فِيهَآ اَحْقَابًا
وَمَآ اُنْزِلَ	اَسْمَآءُ	مَآئِدَةً	وَلَآ اَنْتُمْ
مَآ اَوْحٰى	حَآفِّينَ	مَآ اَنْتَ	مَآ اَغْنٰى

ASSORTED EXERCISES (5)

• Please recite carefully the following examples from
the Qur'ān that contain *the signs of longer madd*.

بِالَّذِىٓ اُوحِىَ	يَتَسَآءَلُونَ	وَمَآ اَرْسَلْنَاكَ	قَالُوٓا اِنَّا
اَلَّتِىٓ اَحْصَنَتْ	هُوَ الَّذِىٓ اَرْسَلَ	رُحَمَآءُ	اَشِدَّآءُ
بِمَآ اَسْلَفْتُمْ	دَآئِبَيْنِ	اَلْحَآقَّةُ	بِشُرَكَآئِهِمْ
رَبِّىٓ اَمَداً	اِنِّىٓ اَعْلَنْتُ	فَلَآ اُقْسِمُ	عَلَىٰ اَرْجَآئِهَا
تُوبُوٓا اِلَيْهِ	مَآ اُرْسِلْتُ	بِسُوٓءٍ	مَآ اَكْفَرَهُ
شَاقُّوا اللّٰهَ	اٰلْئٰنَ	لَآ اَمْلِكُ	اِنِّىٓ اَعِظُكَ
اِنَّنِىٓ اَنَا اللّٰهُ	وَالضَّرَّآءِ	اٰلْاٰءَ اللّٰهِ	كَمَآ اَخْرَجَكَ

32

THE VARYING RECITATIONS OF THE HOLY NAME "ALLĀH"

The letter ل (*lām*) in the Holy Name "Allāh" can be pronounced in two ways:

- If the vowel sign (*harakah*) of the unpronounced transition *hamzah* sign (the *hamzatu1-wasl** that is un-pronounced) occurs as the *fat-hah* before the letter *lām* in the Holy Name "Allāh," that *lām* is recited in a hard way (as the "l" in lawyer).
- If the vowel sign (*harakah*) of the letter coming before the word of "Allāh" occurs as *fat-hah* or *dham-mah*, the letter *lām* in the Holy Name "Allāh" is again recited in a hard way.
- However, if the vowel sign (*harakah*) of the letter before the Holy Name "Allāh" occurs as *kasrah*, this time the *lām* is recited in a softer style (as l in lily.)

* Although the *hamzatu1-wasl* can be written as *alif* carrying a *waslah* sign (ٱ), it is usually indicated by a regular *alif* without a *hamzah*. It occurs only at the beginning of a word, which is pronounced when starting with the word, and dropped when continuing. This means that the *alif* is not pronounced but dropped when continuing.

اَللّٰهُ	وَاللّٰهُ	نَصْرُ اللّٰهِ	فَضْلُ اللّٰهِ
قُلِ اللّٰهُ	رَسُولُ اللّٰهِ	اٰيَاتُ اللّٰهِ	يَدُ اللّٰهِ
رَضِيَ اللّٰهُ	وَلَذِكْرُ اللّٰهِ	هُوَ اللّٰهُ	اِنَّ اللّٰهَ
نِعْمَةَ اللّٰهِ	وَعْدَ اللّٰهِ	اِلَّا اللّٰهُ	تَبَارَكَ اللّٰهُ
اَلْحَمْدُ لِلّٰهِ	مِنْ دُونِ اللّٰهِ	مِنْ عِنْدِ اللّٰهِ	مِنْ اٰيَاتِ اللّٰهِ
بِسْمِ اللّٰهِ	بِاِذْنِ اللّٰهِ	بِنِعْمَةِ اللّٰهِ	فِى سَبِيلِ اللّٰهِ

33

LESSON 23

SECTION 7: ARTICULATION OF DISJOINT LETTERS IN THE QUR'ĀN

MUQATTA'AT (DISJOINT LETTERS)

- There are fourteen different *muqatta'at* (disjoint) letters that are found at the beginning of 29 different *sūrah*s in the Qur'ān.

- Surprisingly enough, these letters are not recited according to the usual *harakah* (vowel sounding) system, but just to their original letter sounds. That is to say, each *muqatta'a* letter is read individually just like every single letter is pronounced while reading the alphabet.

- These letters are either in the form of single letters at the beginning of some *sūrah*s or are found in different combinations of up to five disjoint letters at the beginning of other *sūrah*s.

- They are read with prolongation: If a sign of typical *madd* occurs above them, they are prolonged for the duration of two *harakah*s (2-3 seconds); in case of the longer *madd* sign, they are prolonged for the duration of four *harakah*s (3-5 seconds).

حٰم	صٓ	قٓ	نٓ
حَامِيٓم	صَآد	قَاف	نُوٓن
الٓمٓ	يٓس	طٓس	طٰه
اَلِف لَاۤمِيٓم	يَاسِيٓن	طَاسِيٓن	طَاهَا
طٰسٓمٓ	الٓمٓصٓ	الٓرٰ	
طَاسِيٓمِيٓم	اَلِف لَاۤمِيٓم صَآد	اَلِف لَاۤمۡ رَا	
الٓمٓرٰ	كٓهٰيٰعٓصٓ	حٰمٓ عٓسٓقٓ	
اَلِف لَاۤمِيٓم رَا	كَافۡ هَا يَا عَيۡنۡ صَآد	حَامِيٓم عَيۡنۡ سِيٓن قَاف	

34

SECTION 8: SUN AND MOON LETTERS

In Arabic, the consonants are divided into two groups, called the sun letters (*al-hurūfu'sh-shamsiyyah*) and the moon letters (*al-hurūfu'l-qamariyyah*). When the Arabic definite article "*al-*" (ال) is followed by a moon letter, the "*l*" of the definite article is retained; however, the "*l*" of the definite article "*al-*" assimilates to the initial consonant of the following word when it is followed by a sun letter.

LESSON 24 – RECITATION OF MOON LETTERS

- The moon letters, which are fourteen in number and known as "*al-hurūfu'l-qamariyyah*" in Arabic, are ا ، ب ، ج ، ح ، خ ، ع ، غ ، ف ، ق ، ك ، م ، و ، هـ ، ى

- When the definite article "*al-*" (ال) occurs before the moon letters, both letters (ا and ل) in the definite article "*al-*" are articulated.

- In case another letter occurs before the definite article "*al-*" (ال), then the *alif* (ا) is not pronounced, but the *lām* (ل) of the definite article "*al-*" is articulated strongly with a *jazm*.

- Please pay attention to the *alif* letters given in red color that are not pronounced in the following examples.

اَلْعَزِيزُ	اَلْيَوْمَ	اَلْخَالِقُ	اَلْقُرْاٰنُ
اَلْمَرْعٰى	اَلْهَادِى	اَلْاِنْسَانُ	اَلْغَفُورُ
اَلْجَنَّةُ	اَلْعِمَادِ	اَلْبَلَدُ	اَلْكِتَابُ
وَالْعَصْرِ	اَلْمَاءُ	وَالْفَجْرِ	وَالْقَلَمِ
وَالْجِبَالَ	وَالْاَمْرُ	اِلَى الْجَبَلِ	فِى الْبِلَادِ

RECITATION OF SUN LETTERS

- The sun letters (al-hurūfu'sh-shamsiyyah) are fourteen in number.

  They are ، ن ، ل ، ظ ، ط ، ص ، ض ، ش ، س ، ز ، ر ، ذ ، د ، ث ، ت

- When the definite article "al-" (ال) occurs before the words beginning with these letters, only alif is pronounced. The "l" (ل) of the definite article is not pronounced but assimilates to the following consonant, resulting in a doubled consonant with a shaddah.

- In case another letter occurs right before the definite article "al-", both letters (ا and ل) of the article are unpronounced and the following sun letter is doubled with a shaddah.

- Please pay attention to the alifs (ا) and lāms (ل) that are not pronounced in the following examples.

اَلشَّمْسُ	اَلسَّمَاءُ	اَلدِّينُ	اَلرَّحْمَنُ
اَلذَّاكِرُ	اَلطَّالِبُ	اَلزَّكَوةَ	اَلظُّلُمَاتُ
اَلرَّجِيمِ	اَلصِّرَاطَ	اَلنَّاسُ	اَلدُّنْيَا
اَلسَّمِيعُ	اَلشَّاكِرُ	اَلصَّلَوةَ	فِي الصُّدُورِ
مِنَ النُّورِ	وَالضُّحَى	وَالَّيْلِ	مِنَ الظُّلُمَاتِ
وَالزَّيْتُونِ	وَالتِّينِ	وَالطُّورِ	مِنَ الثَّمَرَاتِ

ASSORTED EXERCISES (6)

• Please recite carefully the following examples from
the Qur'ān that contain *sun* and *moon* letters.

وَالسَّلْوٰى	اَلْقَى السَّامِرِىُّ	مِنَ الرِّجَالِ	مِنَ الصَّيْدِ
تِلْكَ الْجَنَّةُ	صَادِقُ الْوَعْدِ	وَالشَّيَاطِينَ	رَبُّ السَّمٰوَاتِ
وَهَنَ الْعَظْمُ	فِى الْمَهْدِ	مِنَ الْبَشَرِ	وَالْبَاقِيَاتُ
اَهْلَ الْكِتَابِ	مِنَ الصَّادِقِينَ	كَالْجِبَالِ	مِنَ الْمِحْرَابِ
اَلسَّمِيعُ الْعَلِيمُ	جَاءَ السَّحَرَةُ	وَاَقِيمُوا الصَّلاةَ	اَحْكَمُ الْحَاكِمِينَ
وَالسَّابِقُونَ	يَوْمَ الْقِيَامَةِ	يَا اَيُّهَا النَّاسُ	اِلَّا الظَّنَّ
بِذَاتِ الصُّدُورِ	وَالنَّبِيُّونَ	مِنَ الْخَاسِرِينَ	هُوَ التَّوَّابُ

ASSORTED EXERCISES (7)

• Please recite carefully the following examples from
the Qur'ān that have similar sounds but are pronounced differently.

عَلِيمٌ	اَلِيمٌ	وَالسَّلَامُ	اَلصَّلَاةُ
سَوْطَ	فَصَبَّ	اَهْوَالُ	اَحْوَالٌ
مُصَفًّى	عَسَلٍ	وَيُثَبِّتْ	يَنْصُرْكُمْ
سَعِيرًا	ثُبُورًا	عَمَّا	وَاَمَّا
طَائِفَةٌ	وَقَالَتْ	اُوتُوا	عَذَابٌ
يَكُونُ	يَقُومُ	ظَلَمُوا	اِذْ
ضُرٍّ	ظَلَّ	خَاسِرِينَ	حَاسِبِينَ

"Be aware that it is in the remembrance of, and whole-hearted devotion to Allāh, that hearts find rest and contentment."

(Ra'd 13:28)

CHAPTER 2

INTRODUCTION TO QUR'ĀN RECITATION AND THE DAILY PRAYERS (*SALĀH*)

HELPFUL TIPS FOR THE HOLY QUR'ĀN AND ITS RECITATION

Mushaf (A Copy of the Qur'ān):

Mushaf is the specific term used for the printed form of the Holy Qur'ān we hold in our hands as a single-volume book between covers.

Isti'ādhah (Seeking Allāh's Protection):

Before beginning to recite the Qur'ān, one recites the *isti'ādhah* (also referred to as the *"ta'awwudh"*), which is a prayer for Allāh's protection and help against evil suggestions from Satan. It is the phrase of saying, اَعُوذُ بِاللهِ مِنَ الشَّيْطَانِ الرَّجِيم each time before starting the recitation of the Holy Qur'ān. It means, "I seek refuge in Allāh from Satan, the eternally rejected."

Basmalah:

Basmalah is the expression بِسْمِ اللهِ الرَّحْمٰنِ الرَّحِيم. It means "In the Name of Allāh, the All-Merciful, the All-Compassionate."

It is Sunnah to recite both the *isti'ādhah* and the *basmalah* before starting the recitation of the Holy Qur'ān. While one pronounces the *basmalah* at the beginning of each *sūrah*; the exception is the Sūratu't-Tawbah, where only the *isti'ādhah* is recited without the *basmalah*. In case one recites verses from the middle of any *sūrah*, he or she may start either with the *basmalah* or with the *isti'ādhah*.

Juz' (Part):

Every twenty pages of the Holy Qur'ān is termed as one *juz'* (part). As the Holy Qur'ān consists of 600 pages, there are thirty parts in the Holy Qur'ān.

Hizb (Quarter):

Every *juz'* is subdivided into four quarters to facilitate Muslims to memorize or read the Qur'ān by heart more easily. Each quarter is called a *hizb*. There are 120 *hizb*s in the Holy Qur'ān.

Sūrah (Chapter):

The Holy Qur'ān consists of 114 chapters. Each chapter is called a *sūrah*.

Āyah (Verse):

Each of the divine verses of the Holy Qur'ān is called an *āyah*. The independent verses have a certain beginning and end. The lengths of verses may vary from a single letter, to a word, a sentence, some sentences, or sometimes a whole page.

Though the exact number of verses in the Qur'ān may change, depending on different categorizations, there are more than 6000 verses in the Holy Qur'ān.

Meccan and Medinan Āyahs:

According to the commonly accepted definition, the verses revealed before the Hijrah (Emigration of the Prophet to Medina) are called as Meccan, and those revealed after the Hijrah are called Medinan verses. The locations where the *āyah*s were revealed are indicated in the headings of the *sūrah*s.

Sajdatu't-Tilāwah (The Prostration of Recitation):

 There are fourteen different places in the Holy Qur'ān that contain the verses of prostration. And there are warning signs for prostration on the pages where any of these verses of prostration are written. If one recites or listens to a verse of prostration, it is *wājib*, or necessary, for both the reciter and listener(s) to prostrate at that moment. This prostration is called the *sajdatu't-tilāwah*, or recitation prostration; that is, prostration for Qur'anic recitation.

Someone prostrating for Qur'anic recitation can be in two states: either outside of the Prayer or during it. If one of the verses of prostration is recited during the Prayer, the praying person/people should prostrate as soon as the verse ends. It is notable here that one goes to the prostration position only once not twice. Then the praying person/people shall stand back and continue their Prayer. If one of these verses is recited outside of the Prayers, the listeners should turn their bodies to the *qiblah* direction, say "*Allāhu Akbar*" (without raising their hands up to the ears for *takbir*) while going into prostration. They say "*Subhāna Rabbiyal-A'lā*" three times in the prostration position and rise from the prostration without giving *salām*s to the right and left. The following *āyah* is recited in the standing position:

$$\text{سَمِعْنَا وَاَطَعْنَا غُفْرَانَكَ رَبَّنَا وَالَيْكَ الْمَصِيرُ}$$

The prostration of recitation shall be completed after the recitation of this *āyah*, which means: *"We have heard (the call to faith in Allāh) and obeyed. Our Lord, grant us Your forgiveness, and to You is the homecoming."*

Khatm al-Qur'ān (A Complete Recitation of the Qur'ān):

Reciting the entire Qur'ān from the *mushaf* (by looking at the text of the Qur'ān) or from memory is called as *khatm*.

Prayer after the *Khatm al-Qur'ān*:

This prayer is recited by those who complete reading and/or reciting the entire Qur'ān. The prayer is mostly added to the end of the *mushaf*s. People can read or recite this prayer alone or together as/in congregation. There are varying *khatm* prayers; one can recite any of these prayers and then supplicate to Allāh. There is no an obligatory etiquette or manner of reciting this prayer as it is not a part of the Holy Qur'ān.

Hāfiz – Hāfizah:

The males who have memorized the entire Qur'ān and thus can recite it by heart completely are called as *hāfize*s, and the females are called as *hāfizah*s. Indeed, hundreds of thousands of believers throughout the world have committed the entire Qur'ān to memory and thus taken it to heart. The preservation of the Qur'ān by memorizing and thus reciting it from the beginning to the end by heart, without any errors even in the letters, is one of the miraculous aspects of the Qur'ān. The Qur'ān is easy to memorize for the one who desires to do so. Indeed, Allāh the Almighty made Qur'ān so easy to remember that even young children can memorize it. There are, in fact, many young Muslims who have memorized the Holy Qur'ān as early as the age of 5. Though the period of committing the entire Qur'ān to memory may vary from person to person, it is usually possible to learn the whole Qur'ān by heart on the average of two years.

Qāri' (plural Qurra'):

Qāri' is the person who recites the Holy Qur'ān from the *mushaf* or from memory proficiently in any of the seven accepted variant recitations of the Qur'ān with a beautiful voice, distinctly, and in perfect accordance with the rules of *tajwīd*, or the art of reciting the Qurān in style and by giving each letter its full value. Indeed, these outstanding people reveal their broad theoretical and practical *tajwīd* knowledge in their Qur'ān recitation in the most beautiful way.

Imām:

According to the most common usage, an *imām* is the competent person in mosques who is authorized to lead the congregation in Prayer (*Salāh*) and to enlighten, guide and assist people on religious issues. We should also bear in mind that any competent Muslim man can be an *imām* to lead the congregation in Prayer, no matter whether they are officially authorized or not.

Mu'adhdhin (or *Muezzin*—the Caller to the Prayer):

Mu'adhdhin is the person who calls people to the Prayers by reciting the *adhān*, or call to Prayer, recites the *iqāmah*, or the second call for the commencement of Prayer (just before the *fard* Prayer), and calls the *tasbihātus-salāh*, which are recited right after the Prayers as a supplement to the Prayer and in remembrance of Allāh.

SHORT *SŪRAH*S FROM THE QUR'ĀN

A practicing Muslim who prays five times a day may recite a portion from any part of the Qur'ān during the Prayer. This being the case, Muslims mostly prefer to recite particular short *sūrah*s or certain passages from the Qur'ān. In the course of time, people have started to call these *sūrah*s as short *sūrah*s. A Muslim is expected to memorize at least these *sūrah*s and Qur'anic passages, so that he or she might not have difficulty with his or her Prayers.

Sūratu'l-Fātihah

This *surah* of seven verses is called Sūratu'l-Fātihah (The Opening) because it is the opening *surah* of the Qur'ān. It was revealed during the early Mecca period of Prophet Muhammad's Messengership.

1. In the Name of Allāh, the All-Merciful, the All-Compassionate.
2. All praise and gratitude (whoever gives them to whomever for whatever reason and in whatever way from the first day of creation until eternity) are for Allāh, the Lord of the worlds,
3. The All-Merciful, the All-Compassionate,
4. The Master of the Day of Judgment.
5. You alone do We worship, and from You alone do we seek help.
6. Guide us to the Straight Path,
7. The Path of those whom You have favored, not of those who have incurred (Your) wrath (punishment and condemnation), nor of those who are astray.

Sūratu'l-Baqarah (2:1–5)

This *sūrah* of 286 verses takes its name from the story of the cow (verses 67–71) which the Children of Israel was asked to sacrifice upon their sanctification of calf. It began to be revealed just after the Emigration of Prophet Muhammad to Medina and continued to be revealed over almost ten years until the entire *sūrah* was completed.

In the Name of Allāh, the All-Merciful, the All-Compassionate

1. Alif. Lām. Mīm.

2. This is the (most honored, matchless) Book: there is no doubt about it (its Divine authorship and that it is a collection of pure truths throughout); a perfect guidance for the Allāh-revering, pious, who keep their duty to Allāh:

3. Those who believe in the Unseen, establish the Prayer in conformity with its conditions, and out of what We have provided for them (of wealth, knowledge, power, etc.,), they spend (to provide sustenance for the needy and in Allāh's cause, purely for the good pleasure of Allāh and without placing others under obligation).

4. And those who believe in what is sent down to you, and what was sent down before you (such as the Torah, Gospel and Psalms, and the Scrolls of Abraham); and in the Hereafter they have certainty of faith.

5. Those (illustrious ones) stand on true guidance (originating in the Qur'ān) from their Lord; and they are those who are the prosperous.

سُورَةُ الْبَقَرَةِ الْاٰيَةُ ٢٥٥
اٰيَةُ الْكُرْسِيُّ

بِسْمِ اللهِ الرَّحْمٰنِ الرَّحِيمِ ۞ اللهُ لَا اِلٰهَ اِلَّا هُوَ الْحَىُّ الْقَيُّومُ لَا تَأْخُذُهُ سِنَةٌ وَلَا نَوْمٌ لَهُ مَا فِى السَّمٰوٰتِ وَمَا فِى الْاَرْضِ مَنْ ذَا الَّذِى يَشْفَعُ عِنْدَهُ اِلَّا بِاِذْنِهِ يَعْلَمُ مَا بَيْنَ اَيْدِيهِمْ وَمَا خَلْفَهُمْ وَلَا يُحِيطُونَ بِشَىْءٍ مِنْ عِلْمِهِ اِلَّا بِمَا شَاءَ وَسِعَ كُرْسِيُّهُ السَّمٰوٰتِ وَالْاَرْضَ وَلَا يَؤُدُهُ حِفْظُهُمَا وَهُوَ الْعَلِىُّ الْعَظِيمُ

Āyātu'l-Kursiyy (al-Baqarah 2:255)

In the Name of Allāh, the All-Merciful, the All-Compassionate

Allāh, there is no deity but He; the All-Living, the Self-Subsisting (by Whom all subsist). Slumber does not seize Him, nor sleep. His is all that is in the heavens and all that is on the earth. Who is there that will intercede with Him save by His leave? He knows what lies before them and what lies after them (what lies in their future and in their past, what is known to them and what is hidden from them); and they do not comprehend anything of His Knowledge save what He wills. His Seat (of dominion) embraces the heavens and the earth, and the preserving of them does not weary Him; He is the All-Exalted, the Supreme.

Sūratu'l-Fīl
This *sūrah* of five verses was revealed in Mecca.

In the Name of Allāh, the All-Merciful, the All-Compassionate

1. Have you considered how your Lord dealt with the people of the Elephant?
2. Did He not bring their evil scheme to nothing?
3. He sent down upon them flocks of birds (unknown in the land),
4. Shooting them with bullet-like stones of baked clay (an emblem of the punishment due to them);
5. And so He rendered them like a field of grain devoured and trampled.

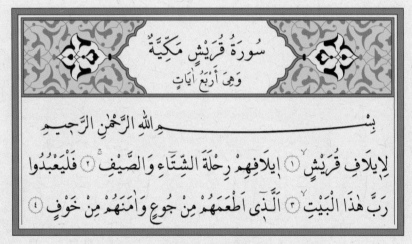

Sūrah Quraysh
This *sūrah* of four verses was revealed in Mecca.

In the Name of Allāh, the All-Merciful, the All-Compassionate

1. (At least) for (Allāh's constant) favor of concord and security to the Quraysh,
2. Their concord and security in their winter and summer journeys,
3. Let them worship the Lord of this House (the Ka'bah),
4. Who has provided them with food against hunger, and made them safe from fear.

Sūratu'l-Mā'ūn

This *surah* of seven verses was revealed in Mecca.

In the Name of Allāh, the All-Merciful, the All-Compassionate

1. Have you ever considered one who denies the Last Judgment?
2. That is he who repels the orphan,
3. And does not urge the feeding of the destitute.
4. And woe to those worshippers (denying the Judgment),
5. Those who are unmindful in their Prayers,
6. Those who want to be seen and noted (for their acts of worship),
7. Yet deny all assistance (to their fellow-men).

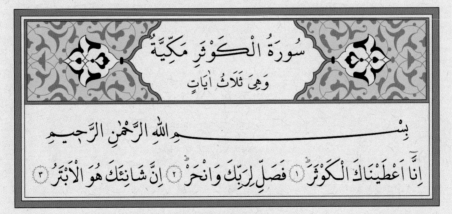

Sūratu'l-Kawthar

This *surah* of three verses was revealed in Mecca.

In the Name of Allāh, the All-Merciful, the All-Compassionate

1. We have surely granted you (unceasing) abundant good;
2. So pray to your Lord, and sacrifice (for Him in thankfulness).
3. Surely it is the one who offends you who is cut off (from unceasing good, including posterity).

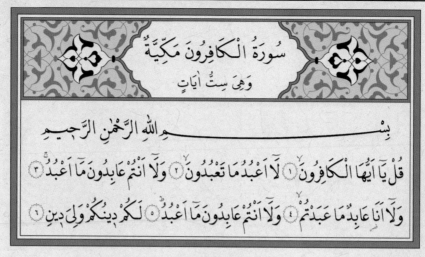

Sūratu'l-Kāfirūn
This *sūrah* of six verses was revealed in Mecca.

In the Name of Allāh, the All-Merciful, the All-Compassionate

1. Say: "O you unbelievers (who obstinately reject faith)!
2. "I do not, nor ever will, worship that which you worship.
3. "Nor are you those who ever worship what I worship.
4. "Nor am I one who do and will ever worship that which you have ever worshipped.
5. "And nor are you those who do and will ever worship what I ever worship.
6. "You have your religion (with whatever it will bring you), and I have my religion (with whatever it will bring me).

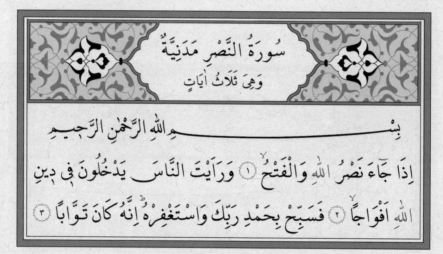

Sūratu'n-Nasr
This *sūrah* of three verses was revealed in Medina.

In the Name of Allāh, the All-Merciful, the All-Compassionate

1. When Allāh's help comes, and victory (which is a door to further victories),
2. And you see people entering Allāh's Religion in throngs,
3. Then glorify your Lord with His praise, and ask Him for forgiveness, for He surely is One Who returns repentance with liberal forgiveness and additional reward.

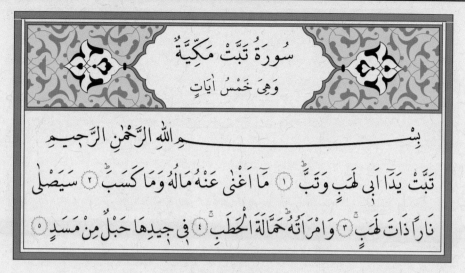

Sūrah Tabbat

This *sūrah* of five verses was revealed in Mecca.

In the Name of Allāh, the All-Merciful, the All-Compassionate

1. May both hands of Abū Lahab be ruined, and is ruined himself!
2. His wealth has not availed him, nor his gains.
3. He will enter a flaming Fire to roast;
4. And (with him) his wife, carrier of fire-wood (and of evil tales and slander),
5. Around her neck will be a halter of strongly twisted rope.

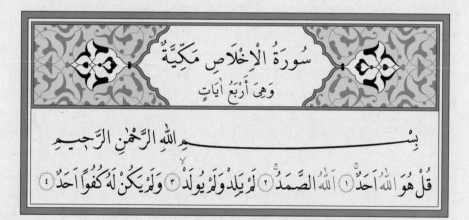

Sūratu'l-Ikhlās

This *sūrah* of four verses was revealed in Mecca.

In the Name of Allāh, the All-Merciful, the All-Compassionate

1. Say: "He – (He is) Allāh, (Who is) the Unique One of Absolute Oneness.
2. "Allāh – (Allāh is He Who is) the Eternally-Besought-of-All (Himself being in need of nothing).
3. "He begets not, nor is He begotten.
4. "And comparable to Him there is none."

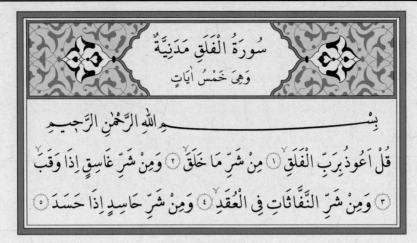

Sūratu'l-Falaq

This *sūrah* of five verses was revealed in Mecca.

In the Name of Allāh, the All-Merciful, the All-Compassionate

1. Say: "I seek refuge in the Lord of the daybreak,
2. "From the evil of what He has created;
3. "And from the evil of the darkness (of night) when it overspreads;
4. "And from the evil of the witches who blow on knots (to cast a spell);
5. "And from the evil of the envious one when he envies."

Sūratu'n-Nās

This *sūrah* of six verses was revealed in Mecca.

In the Name of Allāh, the All-Merciful, the All-Compassionate

1. Say: "I seek refuge in the Lord of humankind,
2. "The Sovereign of humankind,
3. "The Deity of humankind,
4. "From the evil of the sneaking whisperer (the Satan),
5. "Who whispers into the hearts of humankind,
6. "Of jinn and humankind."

PRAYERS RECITED DURING THE PERFORMANCE OF DAILY PRAYERS

The short prayers we ought to recite after starting the Prayer with the opening *takbīr* (by raising the hands up to the ears and saying "*Allāhu Akbar*") are listed below in the order of their recitation in the Prayer. A Muslim person should commit them to memory and recite them by heart for a complete and perfect Prayer. Reciting some of these prayers in the Prayer is a sunnah act of the Prophet while reciting some others are *wājib*, or necessary.

Subhānaka:

سُبْحَانَكَ اللّٰهُمَّ وَبِحَمْدِكَ ۞ وَتَبَارَكَ اسْمُكَ ۞ وَتَعَالَى جَدُّكَ ۞
(وَجَلَّ ثَنَاؤُكَ) وَلَا اِلٰهَ غَيْرُكَ ۞

The part of this prayer given in red is recited only during the Funeral Prayer.

"Glory be to You, O Allah, and to You is the praise. Blessed is Your Name and most high is Your honor. There is no deity besides You."

at-Tahiyyāh

اَلتَّحِيَّاتُ لِلّٰهِ وَالصَّلَوَاتُ وَالطَّيِّبَاتُ ۞ اَلسَّلَامُ عَلَيْكَ اَيُّهَا النَّبِيُّ وَرَحْمَةُ
اللّٰهِ وَبَرَكَاتُهُ ۞ اَلسَّلَامُ عَلَيْنَا وَعَلٰى عِبَادِ اللّٰهِ الصَّالِحِينَ ۞ اَشْهَدُ اَنْ لَا اِلٰهَ
اِلَّا اللّٰهُ ۞ وَاَشْهَدُ اَنَّ مُحَمَّداً عَبْدُهُ وَرَسُولُهُ ۞

"Eternity and all dominion is Allah's, and from Him are all blessings and benedictions. Peace be upon you O the [greatest] Prophet, and Allah's mercy and gifts. Peace be also upon us and Allah's righteous servants. I bear witness that there is no deity but Allah, and I also bear witness that Muhammad is His servant and Messenger."

Salawāt – 1

اَللّٰهُمَّ صَلِّ عَلٰى سَيِّدِنَا مُحَمَّدٍ وَعَلٰى اٰلِ سَيِّدِنَا مُحَمَّدٍ ۞ كَمَا صَلَّيْتَ عَلٰى
سَيِّدِنَا اِبْرٰهِيمَ ۞ وَعَلٰى اٰلِ سَيِّدِنَا اِبْرٰهِيمَ ۞ اِنَّكَ حَمِيدٌ مَجِيدٌ ۞

"O Allah, bestow Your blessings upon our master Muhammad and the Family of Muhammad, as You bestowed Your blessings upon Abraham and the Family of Abraham. Assuredly, You are All-Praised, All-Illustrious."

Salawāt – 2

اَللّٰهُمَّ بَارِكْ عَلَى سَيِّدِنَا مُحَمَّدٍ وَعَلَى اٰلِ سَيِّدِنَا مُحَمَّدٍ ۞ كَمَا بَارَكْتَ عَلَى

سَيِّدِنَا إِبْرٰهِيمَ وَعَلَى اٰلِ سَيِّدِنَا إِبْرٰهِيمَ ۞ إِنَّكَ حَمِيدٌ مَجِيدٌ ۞

"O Allah, send Your abundant gifts and favors unto our master Muhammad and the Family of Muhammad, as You sent them unto Abraham and the Family of Abraham. Assuredly, You are All-Praised, All-Illustrious."

Rabbanā Ātinā

رَبَّنَا اٰتِنَا فِي الدُّنْيَا حَسَنَةً وَفِي الْاٰخِرَةِ حَسَنَةً وَقِنَا عَذَابَ النَّارِ ۞

"O our Lord! Grant us goodness in this world and in the Hereafter and protect us from the punishment of the fire." (al-Baqarah 2:201)

Rabbanāghfirlī

رَبَّنَا اغْفِرْ لِي وَلِوَالِدَيَّ وَلِلْمُؤْمِنِينَ يَوْمَ يَقُومُ الْحِسَابُ ۞

O our Lord! Grant forgiveness to me when the Final Day of Judgment comes, and to my parents and to the believers." (Ibrāhīm 14:41)

Qunut – 1

اَللّٰهُمَّ إِنَّا نَسْتَعِينُكَ وَنَسْتَغْفِرُكَ وَنَسْتَهْدِيكَ ۞ وَنُؤْمِنُ بِكَ وَنَتُوبُ

إِلَيْكَ ۞ وَنَتَوَكَّلُ عَلَيْكَ ۞ وَنُثْنِى عَلَيْكَ الْخَيْرَكُلَّهُ ۞ نَشْكُرُكَ وَلَا

نَكْفُرُكَ ۞ وَنَخْلَعُ وَنَتْرُكُ مَنْ يَفْجُرُكَ ۞

"O Allah! We ask You for help, forgiveness, and guidance. We believe in You and turn to You in repentance for our sins, and place our trust in You. We praise You by attributing all good to You, and thank You, and never feel ingratitude to You. We reject and cut our relations with those who are in constant rebellion against You."

اَللّٰهُمَّ اِيَّاكَ نَعْبُدُ ۞ وَلَكَ نُصَلِّى وَنَسْجُدُ ۞ وَاِلَيْكَ نَسْعَى وَنَحْفِدُ ۞ نَرْجُو رَحْمَتَكَ وَنَخْشَى عَذَابَكَ ۞ اِنَّ عَذَابَكَ بِالْكُفَّارِ مُلْحِقٌ ۞

"O Allah, You alone do we worship, and we pray and prostrate for You alone. We endeavor in Your way to obtain Your good pleasure and approval. We hope and expect Your Mercy and fear Your chastisement, for Your chastisement is to surround the unbelievers."

"(He) taught human what he did not know."

(Al-'Alaq 96:5)

TAKBĪRS (Declaring the Greatness of Allāh), TASBĪHS (Glorifying Allāh) AND TAHMĪDS (Praising Allāh) RECITED DURING THE PERFORMANCE OF DAILY PRAYERS

The expressions to be said at the beginning, during, and at the end of the Prayers are listed below, in the order of saying them during the performance of the Prayers.

- While starting the Prayer (with the opening *takbīr*) and after each *rukn* (essential ingredients or parts of the Prayer), we say the *takbīr* of اَللّٰهُ اَكْبَرُ. This *takbīr* means, "Allāh is the All-Great!"

- In the bowing position (*rukū'*), we say سُبْحَانَ رَبِّيَ الْعَظِيمِ, at least three times. This *tasbīh* means, "All-Glorious is my Lord, the Mighty."

- While rising from the bowing position (*rukū'*), we say سَمِعَ اللّٰهُ لِمَنْ حَمِدَهُ for only one time. This *tahmīd* means, "Allāh hears him who praises Him."

- When we are fully upright (i.e. after reaching *qiyām*, or the standing position), we say رَبَّنَا لَكَ الْحَمْدُ only for once. This *tahmīd* means, "Our Lord, praise is Yours!"

- In the prostration position (in both prostrations), we say سُبْحَانَ رَبِّيَ الْاَعْلٰى at least three times. This *tasbīh* means, "All-Glorious is my Lord, the Most High."

- At the end of Prayer, we give *salām*s (peace greetings), saying اَلسَّلَامُ عَلَيْكم وَرَحْمَةُ اللّٰه while turning our head to the right and then the left (both times). This means, "Peace be upon you, and Allāh's Mercy (be upon you)."

In this way, the Prayer performance shall be completed.

The recitations following the performance of the Prayer (*tasbihātu's-salāh*) start right after one gives the *salām*s to the right and left.

- First of all,

اَللّٰهُمَّ اَنْتَ السَّلَامُ وَمِنْكَ السَّلَامُ ۞ تَبَارَكْتَ يَاذَا الْجَلَالِ وَالْاِكْرَامِ ۞

is recited after giving *salām* on completion of the *fard* Prayer. The meaning of this prayer is as follows: "O my Allāh, You are the All-Peaceful, and from You is all peace. You are the All-Blessed and One bestowing blessings, O One of Majesty and Munificence."

- If there is the sunnah Prayer after the *fard* Prayer, the sunnah Prayer is performed. Then we say عَلَى رَسُولِنَا صَلَوَاتٌ. The meaning of this prayer is as follows: "May Allāh's peace and blessings be upon our Prophet (Muhammad)." Following this, we call for blessings and peace upon our dear Prophet by saying,

اَللّٰهُمَّ صَلِّ عَلَى سَيِّدِنَا مُحَمَّدٍ وَعَلَى اٰلِ سَيِّدِنَا مُحَمَّدٍ

which means, "O Allāh! Bestow Your blessings and peace upon our master Muhammad and upon his Family." Then we say

سُبْحَانَ اللّٰهِ وَالْحَمْدُ لِلّٰهِ وَلَا اِلٰهَ اِلَّا اللّٰهُ وَاللّٰهُ اَكْبَرُ ۞

وَلَا حَوْلَ وَلَا قُوَّةَ اِلَّا بِاللّٰهِ الْعَلِيِّ الْعَظِيمِ ۞

The meaning of this prayer is as follows: "All-Glorified is Allāh, in that He is absolutely exalted above having any defects, needs, and partners; all praise and gratitude is due to and for Allāh; there is no deity but Allāh; Allāh is the All-Great; None has the majesty and none has power to sustain except Allāh, Who is the All-Exalted and the All-Magnificent."

Following this, we recite silently the *Āyat al-Kursiyy* (the Verse of the Throne).

- After reciting the Āyat al-Kursiyy we recite:

  33 times سُبْحَانَ اللهِ (All-Glorified is Allāh),

  33 times اَلْحَمْدُ لِلّٰهِ (All praise and gratitude is for Allāh),

  33 times اَللّٰهُ اَكْبَرُ (Allāh is the All-Great).

- Then we recite

  لَا اِلٰهَ اِلَّا اللهُ وَحْدَهُ لَا شَرِيكَ لَهُ ۞ لَهُ الْمُلْكُ وَلَهُ الْحَمْدُ وَهُوَ عَلٰى كُلِّ شَيْءٍ قَدِيرٌ ۞ سُبْحَانَ رَبِّيَ الْعَلِيِّ الْأَعْلَى الْوَهَّابِ ۞

  which means: "There exists no deity but Allāh; Allāh is One, Allāh has no partners; Allāh has the absolute ownership and dominion; and Allāh is the All-Powerful; I glorify my Lord, the All-Munificent."

- Finally, we raise our hands to make *du'ā*. We can pray to Allāh, ask for forgiveness and mercy from Him, or say our private prayer(s). Here, we can of course pray in our own language and in our own words to our hearts content.

Adhan is a divine call that is made at the beginning of each prescribed Prayer's time and invites Muslims to the daily Prayers five times a day. It is, at the same time, a form of worship and a way of glorifying our Lord. *Adhan*s are commonly called out aloud from a high place (on the minarets of mosques) by the *mu'adhdhin*s who are officially in charge. *Adhan* is one of the collective symbols or marks of Islam.

When it is time for Prayer and there is no mosque in the vicinity, one of the Muslims praying in congregation ought to stand up and call the *adhan* audibly with an enchanting voice. Likewise, even if a Muslim man is performing the Prayer alone, he still should call the *adhan* before starting to perform the Prayer. In addition, the *iqāmah* is sunnah for men only, called out either by the *mu'adhdhin* or the Muslim man praying alone, before starting the *fard* Prayer. The words of the *adhan* and the *iqāmah* are the same other than an additional expression in the *iqāmah*. You can see that difference on the following page.

اَللّٰهُ اَكْبَرُ اللّٰهُ اَكْبَرُ  اَللّٰهُ اَكْبَرُ اللّٰهُ اَكْبَرُ

"Allāh is the All-Great" (four times)

اَشْهَدُ اَنْ لَا اِلٰهَ اِلَّا اللّٰهُ  اَشْهَدُ اَنْ لَا اِلٰهَ اِلَّا اللّٰهُ

"I bear witness that there is no deity but Allāh" (twice)

اَشْهَدُ اَنَّ مُحَمَّداً رَسُولُ اللّٰهِ  اَشْهَدُ اَنَّ مُحَمَّداً رَسُولُ اللّٰهِ

"I bear witness that Muhammad is the Messenger of Allāh" (twice)

حَىَّ عَلَى الصَّلَاةِ  حَىَّ عَلَى الصَّلَاةِ

"Come to the Prayer" (twice)

حَىَّ عَلَى الفَلَاحِ  حَىَّ عَلَى الفَلَاحِ

"Come to salvation" (twice)

اَلصَّلَاةُ خَيْرٌ مِنَ النَّوْمِ  اَلصَّلَاةُ خَيْرٌ مِنَ النَّوْمِ

"The Prayer is better than sleep"

(recited only during the *adhan* for the dawn Prayer twice)

قَدْ قَامَتِ الصَّلَاةُ  قَدْ قَامَتِ الصَّلَاةُ

"Now, the Prayer is about to begin"

(recited only during the *iqāmah* twice)

اَللّٰهُ اَكْبَرُ اللّٰهُ اَكْبَرُ  لَا اِلٰهَ اِلَّا اللّٰهُ

"Allāh is the All-Great" (twice)

"There is no deity but Allāh" (once)

PRAYERS OFTEN RECITED IN DAILY LIFE

The Prayer Made for Success:

رَبِّ يَسِّرْ، وَلَا تُعَسِّرْ، رَبِّ تَمِّمْ بِالْخَيْرِ

"O my Lord! Ease my task, and do not harden!
O my Lord! Let my task be completed in good!"

The Prayer to Be Read for Parents:

رَبِّ ارْحَمْهُمَا كَمَا رَبَّيَانِي صَغِيرًا

"My Lord, have mercy on them even as they cared for me in childhood." (Al-Isrā' 17:24)

The Prayer to Be Read for Children:

رَبِّ اجْعَلْنِي مُقِيمَ الصَّلَاةِ وَمِنْ ذُرِّيَّتِي رَبَّنَا وَتَقَبَّلْ دُعَاءِ

"My Lord! Make me one who establishes the Prayer in conformity with its conditions, and (likewise) from my offspring. Our Lord, and accept my prayer!" (Ibrāhīm 14:40)

The Prayer Made after Finishing the Meal:

اَلْحَمْدُ لِلّهِ الَّذِي اَطْعَمَنَا وَسَقَانَا وَجَعَلَنَا مِنَ الْمُسْلِمِينَ

"Praise be to Allāh who fed us, gave us drink and made us among the Muslims."

The Prayer after the *Adhan*:

اَللّهُمَّ رَبَّ هذِهِ الدَّعْوَةِ التَّامَّةِ ۞ وَالصَّلَاةِ الْقَائِمَةِ ۞ اٰتِ سَيِّدَنَا مُحَمَّدًا الْوَسِيلَةَ وَالْفَضِيلَةَ ۞ وَابْعَثْهُ مَقَامًا مَحْمُودًا الَّذِي وَعَدْتَهُ ۞ اِنَّكَ لَا تُخْلِفُ الْمِيعَادَ ۞

"O Allāh, Lord of this perfect call (to Prayer) and the Prayer that is about to be performed. Bestow upon our master Muhammad the right of intercession and the rank above the rest of creation, and raise him to the honored station You have promised him. Verily, You never fail in Your promise."

The Traveler's Prayer When Seated in a Vehicle or Mounting a Beast of Burden:

$$\text{سُبْحَانَ الَّذِى سَخَّرَ لَنَا هٰذَا وَمَا كُنَّا لَهُ مُقْرِنِينَ، وَاِنَّا اِلٰى رَبِّنَا لَمُنْقَلِبُونَ ۝}$$

"All-Glorified is He Who has subjugated this to our use. We were never capable (of accomplishing this by ourselves). And surely, to our Lord we are indeed bound to return." (Zukhruf 43:13–14)

The Prayer of *Salātan Tunjīna* (also referred to as *Salātu'l-Munjiya*, which is the call for blessings and peace upon our Prophet recited after the *fard* Prayers in praying to Allāh for salvation)

$$\text{اَللّٰهُمَّ صَلِّ عَلٰى سَيِّدِنَا مُحَمَّدٍ وَعَلٰى اٰلِ سَيِّدِنَا مُحَمَّدٍ ۝ صَلَاةً تُنْجِينَا بِهَا مِنْ جَمِيعِ الْاَهْوَالِ وَالْاٰفَاتِ ۝ وَتَقْضِى لَنَا بِهَا جَمِيعَ الْحَاجَاتِ ۝ وَتُطَهِّرُنَا بِهَا مِنْ جَمِيعِ السَّيِّئَاتِ ۝ وَتَرْفَعُنَا بِهَا عِنْدَكَ اَعْلَى الدَّرَجَاتِ ۝ وَتُبَلِّغُنَا بِهَا اَقْصَى الْغَايَاتِ ۝ مِنْ جَمِيعِ الْخَيْرَاتِ ۝ فِى الْحَيَاةِ وَبَعْدَ الْمَمَاتِ اٰمِينَ يَا مُجِيبَ الدَّعَوَاتِ ۝ وَالْحَمْدُ لِلّٰهِ رَبِّ الْعَالَمِينَ ۝}$$

"O Allāh! Bestow blessings and peace upon our master Muhammad and his Family. For the sake of that blessing and peace save us from all misfortunes and disasters, meet all of our needs, and purify us from all vices, elevate us to highest ranks in Your Sight, enable us to attain highest of goals of all kinds of goodness in this life and the next. Amīn, O Who answers all prayers. All praise is due to Allāh—Lord of the worlds."

The Prayer of *Salātan Tafrijiyah* (The call for blessings and peace upon our Prophet recited in praying to Allāh for bestowing blessings and for dissipation of grief and difficulties)

اَللّٰهُمَّ صَلِّ صَلَاةً كَامِلَةً ۞ وَسَلِّمْ سَلَامًا تَامًّا ۞ عَلَى سَيِّدِنَا مُحَمَّدٍ الَّذِى تَنْحَلُّ بِهِ الْعُقَدُ ۞ وَتَنْفَرِجُ بِهِ الْكُرَبُ ۞ وَتُقْضٰى بِهِ الْحَوَائِجُ ۞ وَتُنَالُ بِهِ الرَّغَائِبُ ۞ وَحُسْنُ الْخَوَاتِمِ ۞ وَيُسْتَسْقَى الْغَمَامُ بِوَجْهِهِ الْكَرِيمِ ۞ وَعَلٰى اٰلِهِ وَصَحْبِهِ فِى كُلِّ لَمْحَةٍ وَنَفَسٍ بِعَدَدِ كُلِّ مَعْلُومٍ لَكَ ۞

"O Allāh! Bestow complete blessings and perfect peace on our master Muhammad, and for his sake may all knots be untied (i.e., all our difficulties be removed), all calamities and agonies prevented, all needs fulfilled, all our cherished aspirations obtained, and a felicitous end to earthly life attained (with faith); and (give us) rain-showering clouds for the sake of the munificent countenance of the Prophet; and (bestow blessings as well) on his Family and Companions in every moment and every breath, as many times as is in Your Knowledge (i.e., unlimited blessings)."